Scopcræft

Grace Campbell

Presentation by *BookLeaf Publishing*

Web: www.bookleafpub.com

E-mail: info@bookleafpub.com

ISBN: 9789358310252

First edition 2023

PREFACE

Scopcræft (which translates to "the poet's art" in Old English) was the name of my poetry portfolio for a creative writing class I took in college. I was nervous to take the class because I didn't think of myself as a very good writer. That class allowed me to write and get feedback and I'll always be glad I took it. Writing poetry (or just writing in general) has always kind of been an outlet for me to get whatever was in my brain out. Some of the poems in this book come from that original poetry portfolio and some are from the notes app on my phone. I will say I don't consider myself a good writer in the slightest, but I enjoy writing as a form of therapy so I continue to do so. I hope you all enjoy Scopcræft!

A Thought

People don't tell you that your 20s are gonna be
so hard
They don't tell you about the friendships you
lose
The relationships you discover
They leave out the hating yourself one moment
And thinking you're the shit the next
There's no how-to manual
You have to learn that shit on your own

I want to truly live not just survive
Experience things fully
Not disassociate my way through the day
Express my emotions, good or bad
And have people understand me
I want to love and be loved
Support and be supported
I want to grow and love myself
This life I've created
But it's hard
It's really fucking hard

Today

Today is the day I take the subway
I don't like subways very much
People packed in like sardines in a can
I don't like sardines. I don't like people
"Then why take the subway?"
The answer is simple: to experience
The thrill of conquering my own fears
The rapid beating of my heart in my chest
The blood rushing to my ears
My knees start to quiver
My hand begin to shake
I want to turn back
I need to turn back

But I can't
I won't

My fears do not own me
I've conquered rollercoasters
Up, up, up, then down
Faster than a runaway train
Spiders frighten me no more
I see them now, I'm fascinated
Clowns? Funny little guys
But the subway?

That crowd of hot, sweaty bodies
Too many people, too little air
Too much anxiety
Maybe tomorrow... No
Today
Today is the day I take the subway

Deconstruction

Compersion and guilt walk hand-in-hand
The Curse of normalized monogamy
I love when others feel love
But for some reason I feel guilty
For receiving love in different ways
I need to deconstruct
How I think
How I feel
How I move within the world
I need to allow myself to feel
Different levels of emotion
Connections without guilt

Apologies

5

I don't like when I don't know what to say
People come to me for comfort
I have no clue what to say
So what comes out of my mouth but "sorry"
"It's not your fault" they say
But I AM sorry
Sorry I can't process my emotions and yours
Sorry I feel useless unless you feel better
Sorry I'm a people pleaser
Sorry that "sorry" is the easiest thing to say

Bodies

Girls are too fat; guys are too buff. At the same time, guys are too fat and girls are too buff. Why do we have this innate desire to compare everybody? Every. Body. We compare ourselves and others to societal images that have no purpose but to make us feel worse about ourselves. The only acceptable time for a girl to be "fat" is when she's carrying a baby. Another body. Bodies fill the earth on which we live. Literally. Others are walking, driving, flying. Some are alive, yet don't move. Some are on screens and we compare ourselves and others to those bodies. Sometimes we compare ourselves so much that we start to hate our own bodies. So we alter them, any way we can, good or bad. Our bodies are different. The colors, shapes, the way we carry ourselves. We continue to compare bodies. Why? It's pointless. We all end up the same way anyway. Six feet under. Bodies.

For CD

Sometimes I miss fish bowls in the closet
I miss the bong in the attic
I miss Tuesday night wings
And Friday night at El Charro
I long for late-night talks
The soccer field, the statue of Abe Lincoln
2 A.M. trips to the gym
Perusing downtown
A simpler time that just made sense
I sometimes forget the little things
But they're with me always

Words

How to say that words are not my strong suit
I find it difficult to find the right words
What constitutes the "right words"?
Is that the people pleaser in me?
That I am constantly searching for the right
thing to say?
Maybe I say nothing at all
No need to search for the right words when you
don't speak

Improv

I'm yes and. Yes I'm sweet and I'm a smartass. Yes I'm nurturing and I'm a bully. I don't ever want to be one thing and that's hard. Because yes I want things and I'm scared. I'm scared of a lot. Especially change, new things. The first time is always scary; the second time is easy. But you don't get a second go at life. That happens in movies and tv shows, yes. But. Not in life. I need let my yes and show. I need to improv a little more. To not have a script in my head keeping me back from my yes and.

lightning, thunder, camera, gun

cameras flash all around
people shouting, directing
walk, pose, walk, pose flash
a smile to hide the pain
of aching feet in high heels
a storm of people
their voices booming
"look here! look here!"
their thunderous voices
and bright flashes of lightning
keep me entranced
the calm before the storm is not calm at all
lightning flashes
and then thunder
i'm terrified as pain courses through me
the storm soothes their hunger for more
a red carpet more red now
lightning, thunder
camera, gun
darkness

The Bible Says

"You shouldn't have gotten that piercing, dear
You know what the Bible says about piercings"
So what? Your ears are pierced
What does the Bible say about you?

"If only y'all knew what the Bible says about
tattoos
You wouldn't have gotten them if you knew"
Jokes on you, I would have gotten one anyway
I might get more just to spite you

"These people wouldn't be out doing all this
If they knew what the Bible says about
homosexuality"
Well, I'm gay. How do you feel about that?
Oh? You don't like it? Fuck you

I've heard all of these before so do you really
need to repeat it?
"Piercings, tattoos, gays, bad"
But what does the Bible say about gossip and
judging people?
Because you do an awful lot of that yourself

Interplay

Emotions are funny
Why do I feel loved one moment
And alone the next?
Why are the highs so high
And the lows so low?
Why do I feel so much
Yet nothing at all?
I want to keep moving forward
Without getting pushed back

To Get Away

I've been wanting to get away
Chicago, St. Louis, Austin, Santa Fe
To drive around and get lost
An adventure to escape the monotony
Taking the long way home
A different street, another road
Just to experience something new
Life with more adventure
With tangents and new paths

An Early Night

Little bumps in the night
They try to be quiet while I sleep
Tap clink thunk
I love every second
Every sound lulls me to sleep
The joy it brings me
I've never been so loved

Us

15

A space of our own
Theirs and theirs cabinets, closets
Two copies of our favorites
Comfortable silences
Trinkets so many trinkets
A DVD of childhood performances each
Half-finished projects
Their technology
My traveling
Our fear and thirst for change
It's what makes us us

Passions

I like people who have a passion
I like when they act on that passion
The capability
The mental capacity
The attention span
To do something like that
To know you want to do something
And doing it
I want to find myself
My passion
I want to become a person I enjoy

Mornings

I enjoy slow mornings
No worries about work
No plans for the day
No rush to get out of bed
Just you and me
The soft kisses
Squeezing each other
Just to feel a little warmth
Silence broken up by
Whispered 'I love you's
These are the best mornings

I Write

When I don't know what to say
Or when there are too many thoughts
When my emotions are at their peak
Or I have a moment to spare

A line or two to get it out
The words don't always flow
A jumbled mess just like my brain
Pen and paper comfort me

It's an outlet for each emotion
The good, bad, and in between
I write not to be heard by others
I write to be heard by me

To Be Continued

My thoughts are always jumbled
There are always a million tangents
No story is told straight through
Derailing the train of thought
Only to get back on a parallel track
This is no different
The thoughts I've had in my head
Past, present, and future
All here in one place
A mess of emotion
Love, anger, and sadness
All present
Will forever be present
This will not be the end
But a new chapter, a new book
A continuation of the story of me

www.ingramcontent.com/pod-product-compliance
Lightning Source LLC
Chambersburg PA
CBHW071255140726
47996CB00007B/2849